INDOOR GARDENING FOR BEGINNERS:

A Comprehensive Guide From A To Z In Everything About Improving Your Skills To Grow Up Vegetables At Home Using Kitchens, Backyards, And Other Indoor Opportunities

by **EMILY BATES**

Table Of Contents

Introduction

If you're reading this introduction, then there is a good chance that you are ready to start your indoor garden, but just do not know yet. Do not worry, and this book covers everything you need to get going and start growing your own fruits and vegetables. But there is also the possibility that you have not decided whether indoor gardening is right for you yet. This is understandable since they are not so many drawbacks to indoor gardening as there are pros. Let's take a look at the good and bad of indoor gardening so you can weigh both sides and decide if it's right for you.

Stop-start with the pros. Indoor gardening allows more people to participate and join the wave of gardening that is sweeping through the culture. Due to lack of access to land to plant a garden outdoors, indoor gardening can be a necessity for those who want to garden. But this need also allows great flexibility. Planting in the ground, you know exactly where your plants need to go. However, an interior garden can be done on a shelf, a dedicated space for a hydroponics system, or even in hanging baskets around the living room. Thus, indoor gardening can actually for a variety of approaches.

They are also able to take complete control of the environment in your garden rises. Since the creation of light to provide heat, setting up fans to keep the air fresh, and organizing lots of water, you are able to tune up your garden in much greater depth when it is inside. If you have a garden for the outdoors, you need a lot of light, and then a cloudy day can do serious damage to your plants. However, an interior garden uses electric lights to simulate the sun, and that means that no matter if it is sunny, cloudy, or raining, your plants are always under your control. This level of control when respected and used

With the intention, also it means you can avoid problems with pests and diseases much easier than it could with a garden outdoors. However, that will take us to our first air too.

The fact that it is easier to pests and diseases should avoid gardening inside does not mean you are not a problem. In fact, when pests lead to an interior garden, it can be even harder to repel them as if they were in the great outdoors. Predatory insects seem even less attractive when looking to release them in your living room, after all! If you go inside the garden, then you need to make sure you keep your garden clean and tidy, well-fed, and adequately protected. All this amounts to more chores on a daily basis. This time the means and energy have to be committed to maintaining the garden, time, and energy you can not feel compelled to give after a long day of work.

Other problems that face indoor gardens are a bit cuter. If you have children or pets, then you could have problems maintaining your garden safe. Children have a tendency to break almost everything they get their hands on, and domestic animals, such as cats, you can use your garden as a litter box or even sick (and possibly die) chewing on plants that are growing. What this means is that if you have children or pets, then you must consider the safety of your garden much more deeply than you would if you were outdoors.

The aim of this book is to take anyone of any level of gardening, and put them on the right path for growing healthy plants. It goes over the basics of choosing the plant, and wherein your home is the best place to plant them. Then take a look at irrigation and different types of lighting and containers. It will also refer to fertilize your plants properly and treat

With common pests that could potentially ruin your plants. More generally, the aim is to cover all aspects of installation, care, harvest, and everything that could happen in the middle.

I want you to come away from reading this book, sure you can grow an indoor garden successfully, even if you've never tried your hand at gardening before.

While an interior garden provides control over environmental factors at play, it can become difficult to keep under control when putting into practice. Ensure that the temperature and lighting your plants need is correct may take longer than you think. This is true even when these elements are automated. Automating your garden is not an excuse to ignore your garden. The biggest blow yet, though, is that even if you take care of them all, even if you make sure to pests battle and keep the environment in check, you still may find that your plants are not as tasty as the of the outdoors and older. You make sure that you deal with all this should properly have to be too big a problem,

Most of the information in this book will generally be applied to most types of plants. However, near the end, let's take a look at some specific varieties of flowers, vegetables/fruits, and herbs and get into the details of caring for each. This section is divided into plant type for easy reference, and to give ideas to the aspiring gardener. In this section, you will find a range of different plants with different levels of difficulty. This should give any skill and level of ambition, something to try!

CHAPTER 1:

Where Does Your Garden Grow Interior?

Working with space

Whene it comes to choosing the right space for your garden, it is essential to consider the amount of sunlight the room receives and the amount of control you have over both the humidity and temperature of the space. These three points are discussed in more detail in a moment but should take them into account when deciding what to use instead. If you find that you will need equipment such as a dehumidifier or lamps to grow, then you need to dedicate a larger space to grow if you can rely on the natural characteristics of space. It may be a good idea to outline the area you are looking to grow and take notes on all these different elements. When you have everything on paper in front of you,

It does you have to rent an apartment or greenhouse only to have an indoor garden. Chances are you have plenty of space available to you at this very second if used correctly. Shelves, windows, hanging plants, which can accommodate an entire orchard in your living room with a little creativity. Of course, if you want to go big, then we will address that as well. But it is important to note that it does not occupy much space to start gardening. You could even extend your garden between rooms if I had to: keep tomatoes in the living room while your lettuce is in the bedroom. The only thing stopping you is your imagination limits. In this section, let's assume that you are looking to make a little bigger this configuration; you simply have to consider the space more objectively. However, note that many of the tips for growing more extensive operations are equally applicable to smaller too.

Regardless of where you choose, you will want to make sure that it can be appropriately configured to keep your plants with minimal exposure to the risk of disease and infestation. Some gardeners like to establish their plants behind security measures, such as an air chamber zipper, to help minimize the risk. This is especially true for those who choose to grow using hydroponics method, but let us focus our attention on plants grown in soil. Since this is the case, our best bet for reducing infection is to make sure we use an area with suitable land and proper ventilation to promote healthy airflow.

Soils may seem an odd choice to focus on considering that the plants are in pots, and thus without touching the ground. There are two reasons why we want to keep in mind pavement. The first is to reduce risk, and this means that you should avoid creating your garden in a carpeted space. On the one hand, carpets can be damaged and even start to grow mold because of spills during irrigation. The mats also capture and hold on to a lot of bacteria and germs, and this is very unhealthy for your plants. Mold is going to be something you have to consider in general when it comes to their plants; for example, it part of the garden maintenance is the removal of dead plant matter, which can then rot and mold and spread of the disease. It is much more difficult to say that there is a problem with your carpet; it is to remove plant matter dropped. Some people do not like creating gardens in a room with a wooden floor because irrigation can cause damage to it as well. However, you can minimize this risk by creating a canvas for your plants to rest. Just make sure that the mat can be easily cleaned, and you have a way to remove spilled water.

The significant recommendations are slate flooring, linoleum or ceramic, although they do not always have the option to choose one of these. It is much more difficult to say that there is a problem with your carpet; it is to remove plant matter dropped. Some people do not like creating gardens in a room with a wooden floor because irrigation can cause damage to it as well. However, you can minimize this risk by creating a canvas for your plants to rest. Just make sure that the mat can be easily cleaned, and you have a way to remove spilled water. The significant recommendations are slate flooring, linoleum or ceramic, although they do not always have the option to choose one of these. It is much more difficult to say that there is a problem with your carpet; it is to remove plant matter dropped. Some people do not like creating gardens in a room with a wooden floor because irrigation can cause damage to it as well. However, you can minimize this risk by creating a canvas for your plants to rest. Just make sure that the mat can be easily cleaned, and you have a way to remove spilled water. The significant recommendations are slate flooring, linoleum or ceramic, although they do not always have the option to choose one of these. However, you can minimize this risk by creating a canvas for your plants to rest. Just make sure that the mat can be easily cleaned, and you have a way to remove spilled water. The significant recommendations are slate flooring, linoleum or ceramic, although they do not always have the option to choose one of these. However, you can minimize this risk by creating a canvas for your plants to rest. Just make sure that the mat can be easily cleaned, and you have a way to remove spilled water. The significant recommendations are slate flooring, linoleum or ceramic, although they do not always have the option to choose one of these.

The airflow is vital for your plants. You probably know that plants can drown when overwatered. It may sound a bit strange to hear, but did you know that plants can suffocate, too? When you're in a stuffy room, you start to overheat and lose your breath, right? This can happen to your plants as well. Its leaves to let go of moisture, almost as if they were sweating. Some of this is perfectly normal; in fact, it is what allows your plants to collect more water from the soil. But if they get too hot, too stuffy, then they can not breathe the air more and begin to wither and die. This should be considered in choosing their growing space. You may be able to fit a few plants and

The necessary lights in the broom closet of yours, but the lack of airflow could go out with a bunch of dead plants. You need to have either a natural airflow that can benefit or provide fans to keep air circulating.

Good air circulation does more than keep your plants alive, though. Ventilation and air circulation see a reduction of bacteria and fungi that can cause harmful diseases, but also help make it harder for pests to take home in their plants. Because of the small size of many garden pests, the airflow will make it difficult for them to control their bodies to earth in their plants. That same breeze that makes it harder for pests to land can help your plant's pollination phase, but most likely will not have to worry about this as it is focused on fruits, vegetables, and herbs. What is more important than assistance with pollination is the fact that a decent breeze will strengthen its plants. Branches grow more durable because of the breeze, and this will promote root growth and lead to better harvests. Plants need CO_2 in the air for better growth.

When in a room with stale air, they will absorb all the CO_2 and then start to suffocate. Healthy airflow will bring plenty of fresh CO_2 and oxygen in the space of growth so you can have plants robust high performance. Besides, the airflow will help keep levels of controlled temperature and humidity. So when you are planning your space, pay attention to how the air moves through the area. If you do not, then you will have to invest in some fans, and they take up space, so the best is to plan early around. Airflow help maintains levels of controlled temperature and humidity. So when you are planning your space, pay attention to how the air moves through the area. If you do not, then you will have to invest in some fans, and they take up space, so the best is to plan early around. Airflow help maintains levels of controlled temperature and humidity. So when you are planning your space, pay attention to how the air moves through the area. If you do not, then you will have to invest in some fans, and they take up space, so the best is to plan early around. Pay attention to how the air moves through the area. If you do not, then you will have to invest in some fans, and they take up space, so the best is to plan early around. Airflow help maintains levels of controlled temperature and humidity. So when you are planning your space, pay attention to how the air moves through the area. If you do not, then you will have to invest in some fans, and they take up space, so the best is to plan early around. Pay attention to how the air moves through the area. If you do not, then you will have to invest in some fans, and they take up space, so the best is to plan early around. Airflow help maintains levels of controlled temperature and humidity. So when you are planning your space, pay attention to how the air moves through the area. If you do not, then you will have to invest in some fans, and they take up space, so the best is to plan early around. So when you are planning your space, pay attention to how the air moves through the area. If you do not, then you will have to invest in some fans, and they take up space, so the best is to plan early around. So when you are planning your space, pay attention to how the air moves through the area. If you do not, then you will have to invest in some fans, and they take up space, so the best is to plan early around.

Finally, we will be talking about the light of the sun further in a moment, but it should be noted here as well. Plants need light; it is more or less a golden rule with all plants grows unless something very significant purpose needs. In considering the space, pay attention to sunlight they will receive. Indoor cultivation which often means they can not rely solely on the light of the sun but have growing purchasing views. Like all teams, they take up space that should be planned for. Electricity produce lights are also eaten, and this means a monetary cost associated with them. Your best bet is likely to use a combination of sunlight and electric lighting. This means that to find out how much space sunsets and then use the lights to give your plants the extra boost they need. For example, tomatoes need at least eight daylight hours. If you can trust the light of the sun for six hours of the day, then you only need to try two or three hours of light through your computer. Gardening in this type often requires flexibility to ensure a delicious harvest.

The use of natural sunlight

When the outdoor garden, it is clear that we rely on the sun on to provide our plants with everything they need. There may be cloudy or rainy days causing problems, but usually not set lights to compensate for these. We give our trust completely to the natural order of things. However, when it comes to indoor gardening, it becomes much more complicated. Our access to the sun depends on windows, doors, and the like. We can still make use of the sun but will take into account more than just placement in the backyard and let nature take its course. In order to make better use of our planet bright orange, take a moment to consider how it moves in relation to your gardening space.

The first thing to remember is that the sun rises in the east and sets in the west. Since this happens every day, we can use this to set up an experiment to see how much sun you can capture the interior. However, in order to do this, you must first calculate what direction faces his apartment or house. One way is to take a compass and see which direction is on every wall. If you do not have a compass, do not worry, you can do it from the comfort of your computer chair. Go to maps.google.com and entry of your address. Click the button and see the satellite view, including view.

A compass in the corner. You can use this to see exactly which way he faces everything and use this to help determine the best location for your garden to get plenty of suns. However, they remain; there is one more important step.

If you live in the Northern Hemisphere, then the winter sun will rise in the southeast, head further south, then set in the southwest. This leaves the sun in the south along the next day. The summer sun will rise in the northeast and travel to the northwest, leaving it on the north side of the house all day. Knowing this, you can judge whether you want to plant north or south. So now we know how the sun travels and what section of the home that will be, but this still does not completely capture all you need. There is one last step you should take into account: the environment that surrounds him.

Drink a looks out of the windows in the space of growth you are considering. If you live in the city, you may have buildings that are blocking out part of the path of the sun; If you live in the country, then you may have trees and plants that give shade cast. Depending on how they block the path of the sun, they could cause major problems. For example, if you have a building that light from the sun reaches its plants for two hours of the day, then this can certainly be harmful to your plants' stops. A the same as you and I have our dream, and our bodies tend to set their rates based on the amount of light around us, so do plants. They lose the light for those hours; it is thought to bedtime.

In taking the time to research the relationship of the sun with space for growth, you will be able to identify potential problems like this ahead of time. A solution to this particular problem would be to invest in some grow lights and an automatic timer. You can set the timer, so the lights are turned fifteen minutes before the sun disappears behind the obstruction, and turn off fifteen minutes after that peeks out. As the arc of the sun changes throughout the year, it is useful to keep track of what you are doing so you can adjust the time as needed. By setting to have a fifteen-minute window overlap, are

Create a safety cushion to ensure that their plants always get the light they need to stay healthy and strong.

Thinking about the temperature and humidity

The final piece to be considered in this planning stage is the temperature and humidity of the space growth. Different plants require different temperatures and humidity levels, which means you may need to consider a second space growth if you are looking to produce something completely out of sync with most of your garden.

That said, it almost certainly can bet that whatever space you choose will need to have more moisture added to it. Plants love things. Do we remember how we mentioned that plants breathe? Pores breathing lose moisture when the air around them dry. This can make plants fill wrinkles and end very quickly. A good rule of thumb when it comes to planting leaves is thicker the plant, which will require less moisture. Humidity for indoor gardening should be about 40% -50%. If you do not know the moisture of the crop area, you can buy a hygrometer in most pharmacies. These handy little devices allow you to control indoor humidity.

Humidity Indicators in hand, check the space growth throughout the day. While entering and only get a single rating can do the trick, it's always better to have an idea of how space changes throughout the day. Space will probably need

To have the moisture added to it, which can be done by creating a humidifier. But do not forget, each new piece of equipment you need to add to your garden space required. It is important to keep this in mind to always reach every floor. Cutting off access to plant almost guarantees that you forget to give you the care you need. With the new humidifier, you can set a timer to keep moisture under control at all times, thanks to the notes you took with a hygrometer.

A large majority of vegetables that are likely to grow will require a temperature of 65-75F. Plants do not die immediately if they are slightly out of your preferred temperature. You can most likely keep alive that wants to grow 65F while those who want to 75F, but performance will reflect this.

Exit, and you take a thermometer inside. There are some that can be programmed to record the temperature at fixed intervals; Such an instrument could be a good investment. As with the humidity, you want to monitor the temperature of your chosen space throughout the day. Obviously, it will fluctuate greatly as the day changes tonight. A thermometer first range allows you to see if you need to add heaters or fans to adjust the temperature of the room. You have to have a fan running, so remember to take the temperature with and without that being active. If it has yet to get the fan, then these numbers can be adjusted later. The important thing is to keep track of them, so you always know exactly what is happening with your plants. This level of care may seem unnecessary,

Soil and nutrients

The soil is where your plants get their nutrients and are, therefore, one of the most important aspects to ensure healthy plants. The floor also presents a unique problem for indoor gardeners who never changes. In contrast to the outdoors, where there are a lot of factors that are constantly cycling nutrients in the soil, inside nutrients is based on you. This usually requires some type of fertilizer or organic fertilizer added to the soil, but it will take over soon enough. For now, let's see pick the best soil.

At the end of this section must understand the importance of soil in your garden and how to get the most out of it. You will also learn about composting and fertilization to maintain its nutrient-rich soil.

What is the difference between soil and dirt"?
A common question for new gardeners is: "What is the difference between soil and dirt"?

The short answer usually comes down to the nutritional content of the medium. Dirt is generally considered that it is the soil without any nutrients in it. If you are going to pick up a handful of dirt that is not easy and coalesce

Unlikely to have any type of microorganisms that live in it. In short, it is not a good home for your plants.

Of soil, on the contrary, it will be rich in both nutrients and microorganisms. A handful of dirt is grouped nicely and retains water much better than normal dirt. If you see organizations such as red worms, then it is a good indication of nutrients from the soil. Creatures how are you will not be able to survive on land devoid of nutrients.

At the start, your garden, buying a bag of soil from a garden shop or home, is usually a safe bet. These are generally high nutritional value and provide an excellent place to start for your plants. It is not advisable to go and grab some dirt from the outside for two main reasons:

1. The nutrient content is unknown; it could be planting your plants in a handful of the dirt devoid of nutrients.

2. It may contain parasites harmful or errors that are unknowingly in his brining home. Not only is flat gross, but these types of parasites that could cause damage to your plants.

For these reasons, the best and safest bet is simply to buy a bag of potting soil. This does not have to be expensive, because even the cheaper varieties are perfectly fine for most growers. DO make sure, however, to buy land for labeling containers for use.

The soil in garden beds made to the outdoors is different from potting soil, not drain properly in containers.

However, most of these soils are not pre-packaged for long-term use. The soil itself is an organic material, and all organic material decomposes with time. Some signs of this are:

• The soil is compressed and appears to almost be the solution. Will be lost that kind of light, fluffy appearance it once had. This makes the soil is packed tightly around the roots depriving the plant of oxygen.

• Drainage is impeded and may notice that it takes time for the soil to dry. In some cases, you may notice some water standing on the floor. This prevents your plants get the water they need and also increases the chances of root rot!

• Mineral salt and accumulates; If you are using a clay pot, you will notice more frequent white stripes around it. This is the salt and other minerals that have seeped into the pot. This is normal in small amounts, but too much can fry and kill the roots of a plant.

To combat this, it is generally a good idea to re-pot your annuals. Simply removing them from their container, wash the old floor, and replant with new soil. This ensures that the earth is good enough for nutrient loading and water to allow the plants to continue growing.

When transplanting, be sure to thoroughly wash pots, especially if they were to the outdoors for any length of time. This avoids any problems with insects or other pests transplantation.

In addition to transplantation, the correct use of fertilizers can also help keep your fresh soil of nutrients. Although it is still an excellent idea to annual transplant,

Compost can help keep the soil fresh amid the operation. Coincidentally, it is also our next topic.

Types of soils

Let talk briefly about soil types as there are a couple you could meet. In general, most plants grow well in potting soil store-bought, but there are individual plants that prefer a different floor. Succulent, for example, prefer a coarser soil is sand and 1/3 drains quickly. By matching the type of soil with care more straightforward to find the plant.

Fertilizer and compost

An essential aspect of healthy plants is to ensure they get enough nutrients. As discussed above, the store-bought potting soil will be chosen usually packed with nutrients, but at some point, be exhausted requiring some assistance. Let the plants sit on the floor that has run out of nutrients is an excellent way to kill your plant.

Proper use of fertilizers can help restore some of these nutrients to your soil, and save the trouble of having to replant so often.

To start, touch left in store-bought, pre-made fertilizer. These are great for most gardeners because they are convenient, quick, inexpensive, and add a lot of nutrients in the soil. That said, there are a few things to consider.

Without Dispersion
In the outdoors, fertilizers, naturally seep into the surrounding soil and spread through the garden. A plant can take what you need during this process, and all the rest to disperse throughout the surrounding soil.
A container inside, however, is not the case. What is placed on the ground it is not stuck without any additional space to filter. Also

The amount of fertilizer can kill the plant in this way, primarily if manure is used based on chemicals. Some General wisdom is to use a part of the recommended amount, up to ¼ of smaller vessels.

This helps prevent over-fertilization but still provides enough nutrients for the plant to survive. To dilute fertilizer, a simple mixture of water to the preferred concentration.

It also does not fertilize too often. This will be specific to the plant, but on average, once every few months is more than enough.

Go Organic

the use of organic fertilizer is also recommended growing inside. This one stops to bring potentially harmful chemicals in your home, but also helps mitigate the risk of unusual fertilizer plants. A good organic fertilizer will be as effective as a chemical. The disadvantage is organic fertilizers are often a bit more expensive.

Slow release or Water Soluble

There are a variety of different types of fertilizers on the market, but for indoor use, the two most popular are water-soluble and slow-release.

Water-soluble fertilizers are mixed right in the shower and mixed with water. This gives a great deal of control over the quantity delivered to the plants and enables the ramp up or back cut power to match cycles plant growth. It also makes it easy to reach your desired level of strength, use less fertilizer, and more water to lower the concentration.

Slow-release fertilizers are placed right on the floor. They are coated with a unique shell that leached manure directly into the ground. These may last several months and are great for the forgetful or busy gardener. Also, they are quite light in terms of actual fertilizer placed on the ground, so the risk of scandalizing plants is too low.

Compost

Not talk about feeding the plants would be complete without the fertilizer!

The compost is made from decaying matter, which can be anything from apple cores daily. When these exotic decays release nutrients in your soil that plants love! Add in the fact that you can make a quality compost discarded items from your home and budget-conscious an excellent fertilizer is done without sacrificing nutrients. The compost is also all-natural, so you get the benefits of an affordable organic fertilizer.

A problem with the indoor composting is the smell. As the compost is made from decaying matter, it frequently has an unpleasant odor. Fortunately, there are ways to help prevent this. Let's take a look at how to start a

Simple but effective that the compost will not make your house smell like garbage.

First, you need to select a container and space to hold it. Find out where you want to host the compost bin (under the sink, in the closet, in your cover, etc.) And pick a container that fits it. The box can be any container, but be sure to drill some holes in the bottom and have some attempt to catch the dirt street. Plastic bags most stores are perfect for this if you have space.

Once you've chosen the container and the location is time to add the ingredients. One important thing to consider is that it is about two parts, per brown, green part.

Brown items include:
- Press
- journals
- Wood Shavings
- Dead leaves
- sawdust

Green objects include:
- Fruit Waste
- ground coffee
- Grass clippings
- General food waste
- Tea Pants

You will want to follow the breakdown above parties to maintain down the smell. A good practice is to bury food in the components "brown" to help mask any odor too. If the scent starts to become a problem, change the ratio of "brown" to "green" to promote "brown" more since these items have no specific odor and mask the smell of food waste. If done well, it should not be any unpleasant odor generator of decomposition.

Also, every couple of days to go through and turn the compost while adding some water. This again helps keep the odor down and also promotes the generation of healthy compost. Once the compost becomes a vibrant brown color, and you can not discern the original contents were, it's time to use it!

When the compost is used, sprinkle on the floor and work on a little. One good thing about compost is that it does not use chemicals aggressive not to damage plants if you add a little too close to the ground.

As the last word, avoid adding any animal droppings, meat, bones, dairy products, fish, or dyed materials. All this can cause harmful compost, attract unwanted pests, odors, and add, unfortunately. It is best to avoid them altogether. Your compost should be of a material herbal, so if it is an animal, stay clear!

CHAPTER 2:

Getting Started Gardening

Now that you have chosen space for your garden, it's time to start gathering all the necessary materials and put them together. We discuss the tools described in the previous chapter, fans, and humidifiers. However, we will mainly be talking about the containers that house our plants, the culture medium living in, and the various tools we use to take care of them and keep them healthy.

At the end of this chapter, you should be able to put together a shopping list for all the items you need to take care of your garden. In creating this list, it is worth noting that we are not looking for supplies needed for growing hydroponic gardens. While hydroponic gardens work perfectly well indoors, with an entirely different set of needs that we are raising plants in this garden. We are getting our hands dirty in the soil like people used to!

Picking the right container for your plants

There are two steps to collect all the plant containers. The first is to consider the size of the container, such as plant needs. First, let's take a quick look at the different sizes and what they are used to grow. But the other step is to consider the material that the container is made of. Once you've figured out what is right for your needs, there will still be the last step you should take into consideration making your list.

Pots they come in all different sizes. At the lower end are small pots 10 inches. At the upper end, they are over 30 inches or 3 gallons at the small end and 30 gallons high. Also, it has 14, 16, 18, and 24 inches pots that are typically used. If you go after unique shapes and designs, then you can end up with oddly shaped pots that do not align with these. In the focus our attention on these sizes, you will be able to see the difference between them and use that knowledge to make an educated guess about what can grow in any strange pots that end with. Trust me, once gardening, people have a tendency to give as gifts boats.

Ten inches: In such a small pot like this, you can only grow an herb like mint or sage. Or you could grow a single strawberry or head lettuce leaf. Could go crazy and grow four turnips or carrots dozen French but that's pretty much it.

Fourteen inches: A cabbage, peas four, one Collard. You can go crazy here and grow carrots, tens of regular size instead of the smaller French rounds. You could probably get away with three heads of a lettuce leaf. Four if you are careful.

Sixteen inches: Now you can really get away with some growing vegetables. It can accommodate everything from before, but now in greater numbers. However, this is still too small for many vegetables.

Eighteen inches: there is a good chance that he is wanted in pots of this size or greater for your garden. This is because one can hold an eggplant, a pepper, a cauliflower, bush tomato, or broccoli. Still, you can only fit one of those because they are larger plants.

Twenty-four inches: You can grow cucumbers, blackberries, raspberries, tomatoes Vining, pumpkin, or even a fig tree in a pot 24 inches. Again, just it is going to be growing one per pot.

Thirty inches: Most likely only be used a container 30 inches if you want to grow very large and heavy plants such as cherry, corn, pumpkins, or rhubarb.

Use this guide to plan what you need pots; you should be able to settle in sizes now. So let's focus our attention on the material. The most popular options are among plastic, wood, terracotta, or ceramic. Each has its advantages and disadvantages. However, you need to ensure that any kind that goes with has been incorporated into the drainage for your plants, not drown.

Right off, you should probably avoid wooden pots, while these are very popular for many producers who have their drawbacks. On the one hand, they slowly break apart over time. They can also rot from water damage, which is not ideal when you consider the number of plants to enjoy your water. Ceramic is a better choice than wood and often looks very beautiful and bright colors. They are excellent for indoor plants, but they are one of the most expensive options.

If you are concerned about the price, terra cotta, or plastic, they might be more affordable than ceramics. Plastic containers are very light, which makes it easier to move your plants. However, this can lead to problems if you are looking to grow heavy plants. Plastic tends to be the cheapest to buy, although they are likely to break equally, if not more, than wooden pots. Cotta, on the other hand, is cheaper than ceramics, but more expensive than plastic. It is also much heavier than plastic. Terracotta pots have a tendency to dry faster than other types, so, if used, they will have to water the plants more often. Of course, if you are growing a few herbs that enjoy drier climates, Regardless of what you go with, you can expect each category to sell in a price range depending on how the assumption that the boat is. You can easily spend a couple of hundred dollars in pots that could be purchased for $ 20 at a cheaper design. Its plant is enjoying a boring container much as they do a pretty, so this is all about what you want rather than what the plant needs.

There is one more thing about the containers that must be addressed. It's a good idea for some smaller buy that can be used for planting seeds. When a seed is planted, it is in a smaller container, and then move to the bigger house when it has grown at a healthy size. Having a little smaller

Containers around is always a good idea. In the same way, pots will end up being given as a gift; people also start giving seeds. You never know when you can have a new vegetable join your garden.

Lighting the way

As everyone knows, lighting is one of the most important aspects of growing healthy plants. Get enough light, and you will have beautiful crops. It is not enough and begins to wilt and look sickly. In this section, we will take a look at all the light things, and learn how to provide adequate lighting for your plants.

While gardening indoors has two sources of light, sun and grow lights. The sun is pretty self-explanatory, a pretty big window is a better gardener friend. It is also free, so definitely use it if you have the choice. The other source of light is the creation of artificial light growth. These can compensate for the lack of natural light and are a great choice. Setting artificial lights, however, can be a bit of a challenge. There are various types and intensities that can be bought, so it can be a bit confusing at the beginning to find out which one is right for you. Not to worry, however, that you covered!

Know your plants

The first step to figuring out your lighting needs is to find out what plants are wanted. While some plants want more than 12 hours of direct light from the sun, other wither under the same conditions. It is important to understand your plants and make sure they get the care they need.

In general, plants that you intend to eat requires lighter. This includes fruits and vegetables, followed by grasses. The plants in these categories are likely to need to 8 hours of bright light, or risk having stunted. That does not mean that the flowers may not need a lot of light, so be sure to understand your specific needs.

On the other hand, many types of common houseplants, such as ficus, can get by with much less light shade and even significant. A peace lily, for example, actually too light fades. This only serves to demonstrate the wide range of lighting needs between plants.

The main point to take here is that light needs can vary greatly between plants, so learn and plan accordingly.

Natural light

The first option that most gardeners will see natural light. This is also a far easier option because it requires no configuration to start.

As noted above, lighting facilities' needs will be different, so make sure that the area receives sufficient daylight plants. It is also important to note that in many places, the intensity of the gems of light in the winter. This means that an area that can receive enough light in summer it does in the winter. Take note of this and adjust accordingly.

Beyond that, there is not really much to do here. Just make sure your plants are receiving enough light, and you're good to go. Where begins the real challenge is when you need to start looking in grow lights, so let's go over now.

To begin with lights

The use of indoor growing lights is an excellent way to supplement or replace sunlight for your plants. Generally behave exactly like the sun, although the amount of time that will be influenced by how strong the light and how far the plant is located.

If you are planning to use the lights for your garden, you are a couple of things to consider, and a couple of different types of light can be found.

Watch your lights

Depending on the lights used (if using them) that can be heated. Warm enough in the fact that it can actually harm your plants. In most cases, you will want to give 12 "-24" of space between the lights and plants. Overall, this allows them to be as effective as possible, cover.

 The largest amount of area, and be far enough to alleviate any concerns heat. In general, incandescent bulbs will emit a lot of heat, and be quite energy inefficient.

For the novice, non-commercial growers, fluorescent lighting is one of the best options. They are common, cheap, and efficient. They do not generate large amounts of heat, so you can safely base closer to plants than their incandescent cousins.

The wavelengths of light understanding

One important thing to consider is the wavelength of light and how it affects plants. Different wavelengths stimulate plants in different ways, and different lights emit light in different amounts. In many cases, a mixture of different wavelengths will provide optimal growth.

Here are some wavelengths that keep the lights want to look to buy.

Red: Promotes flowering and flowering

Blue: Promotes the growth of foliage

White: A mixture of all wavelengths of type

Each of these has different uses, so one may need to mix types depending on your goals.

Incandescent lights

The most basic lights are standard incandescent bulbs. These are your run of the mill bulb. They are hot. When they used these want to place about 24 "of the plant since they can damage the plant.

Many beginners tend to move away from incandescent bulbs because they are easy to spoil and extremely energy inefficient. The saving grace is that they emit red wavelengths that can help promote flowering plants. It will be seen later that complements the nice blue emitted by fluorescent lights. A ratio of 1/3 is incandescent, a good place to start.

Fluorescent lights

These common types of light come in two main types larger tubes and bulbs. The tubes are great for covering large areas, while light bulbs will allow specific target plants.

Another big advantage of these bulbs is their low power consumption and saving money.

Compared to the old fashioned incandescent bulbs, fluorescent use much less energy and last longer, both those that result in cost savings. Also, they release much less heat, which means that you can place closer to the plants that need more intense light without fear of them overheating.

Fluorescent lights emit a lot of blue light, so look for the label "full-spectrum". This will ensure that you get enough to promote the growth of paper for all kinds of plants.

Led lights

LED lights are another great option that comes in many different types. Due to the variety of lights looks specifically for cultivation. This will ensure that the wavelengths are suitable for fostering the growth of plants. There are many common types of LED lights that do not have the appropriate wavelengths, so be sure to choose the right lighting.

High-intensity discharge (HID)

The last option for lighting the lights are HID (high-intensity discharge). These lights are normally used for the enterprise grows, and usually not for recreational growers. While it is not something, you're likely to find, it is good to know that it is an option.

Light placement

Generally, you want the light to be above exposing each side of the plant alike. However, this is not always possible. Even with the light of the sun, you sometimes encounter a side of the plant to get lighter than the other.

In these cases, simply turn the plant to the other side faces the sun.

You may notice that sometimes the plant tends to lean toward the light. If not rotated, this can lead to a weak stem that can cause more.

Complications. A simple rotation helps each side exposed to the ground and keeps it inline growth.

Light timers

While plants need light, also they require dark periods. The plants are subjected to a process called "breathing," which is the opposite of photosynthesis. Unlike photosynthesis, respiration does not require sunlight and, therefore, can be done in the dark. Therefore, it is important to ensure that the plants receive a dark and light cycle, much as they would in the nature of the sun.

If your primary light source is the sun, then this cares you take. Simply leave the plant is overnight to give a period of darkness.

This works perfectly fine for a good number of houseplants common.

If you are using grow lights, a simple way to do this is with a timer light. You can set the timer to be intermittent during certain periods, to give precise control over light and dark times of its plants. Light timers are low cost and are ideal for the gardener to forget to help turn off or turn on the lights.

The ultimate goal here is to mimic what the plant would look like in nature. Look at the natural habitat of plants and to provide them with an appearance similar to that environment.

Common lighting problems

To cap things for this section, we will look at a couple of issues that could be caused by inadequate lighting.

Wilting leaves or Browning: In some cases, wilting or browning leaves may be a problem caused by inadequate lighting. This can be grow lights are very close/hot, or lower light plant receives too much direct sunlight. Note that this can also be problem irrigation, so be careful if you encounter this problem.

Plant tips: This is often caused by more intense lighting to be from one side. Plants often bend light, and this can lead to weakness, and problems stem from future growth. Simply turn the plant every day to maintain constant light.

My plants do not bloom or produce fruit: This is very often the case not receive enough light. Many fruits and vegetables are grown well in low light, but not actually produce any edible pieces. If this is the case, try increasing the time the plant is in the light. If you are using grow lights, try adding more red light or increasing intensity.

All about water

Irrigation is often one of the most vexing parts of growing plants. While we all know the importance of flooding, which can be challenging to know how much is too much or the amount is too small. One of the biggest reasons for less than ideal indoor garden plants is derived from irrigation problems. In this section, we will see how water plants, how to avoid overwatering, and how to avoid common mistakes irrigation.

While all plants require different amounts of water, some general rules can be applied to most plants.

On the one hand, plants are grown in containers usually dry faster than those of the cultivated outdoors. Nor is there room for a houseplant to spread its roots to gain excess water. While one plant to the outdoors can try to fetch water, a houseplant requires the intervention of the gardener to ensure that water. It also has the benefit of rainwater to offset the aid work of you, and the only plant gets from you.

There is also no room for excess water to drain. Outdoors that can pour through the floor but in a container no such luxury. Therefore, it is not essential for water. Overwatering can also be mitigated by adequate support drainage in the pot, as previously discussed.

For most plants, water when the soil is dry to the touch. This is very general but applies to most plants, good general rule. Give the floor a short contact with maybe an inch deep, and water only when dry or nearly so. This is once again, the issue of excess irrigation help, as it prevents watering too often.

As noted, this is very general advice, and while it might work for some plants is essential to understand their needs of plants. Some plants have unique watering needs, so keep that in mind figuring an irrigation program.

How much to water

How much to water the plants depends on many factors? One is the size of the plant, its pot, and the plant itself. A larger plant needs a little more water, for example. As a rule, the soil should be saturated enough, but should not be standing water on top of the floor afterward.

Generally, once there are a little water escapes through, the drain holes have received enough water and should stop watering.

Let's take an in-depth look at the various factors that may influence the amount of water your plant.

Age plant

Plants that are proliferating budding or require more water and energy to sustain its growth that latency or past it's prime. Be sure to provide growing plants with a little extra water to facilitate growth. On the back, be very careful watering older plants as it is more likely than not need much and sit on it if too much is added. You'll also want to check plants often grow back and forth to see if the soil is dry and water when it is.

Time of the year

In growing winter plants, usually, it slows down. This is especially true for plants to receive natural sunlight. As the plants are becoming less that require less water. Many plants go through periods of inactivity in winter, even those in adults indoors. In cases like this, less it is usually more than plants need a little less water.

Humidity

Plants in very humid places need less water, and vice versa. If you are afraid of overwatering but finding the leaves beginning to wither, grab a spray bottle and mist them lightly. This support can encourage plants without adding additional water-saturated soil.

How to know if there is a problem?

Unfortunately, signs of minor and significant irrigation are very similar. The first signal is typically withered leaves. If note that the leaves are beginning to close or faded appearance, give the floor and touch and see whether it is scorched too saturated, this should indicate the direction problems lies.

Some other common symptoms of low / overwatering are:

• Leaves falling off
• Stunted growth
• Discoloration

If any of these symptoms do not panic, some bad watering your plant will not kill immediately. Simply determine which of the problems you are having and then either provide additional water or hold off watering during extra time. If you are actively checking your plants every few days, then you should be able to catch and correct problems before they become a problem with your plants.

While irrigation may seem a little challenge for new gardeners, it is not so bad. In most cases, the soil test is the best option to keep your plants healthy. For most people, it is doing in the habit can be difficult. Many plants die from the owners simply forget to water them.

The best advice is to make part of the plant watering your daily routine perhaps, while coffee is brewing in the morning to turn around and check all.

Your plants to see if they need water. After a while, you will have a good understanding of when and how much to water and be able to take care of your plants like a pro.

Everything else Need You.

Even when the big team everything has been addressed, there will still be several pieces you need to buy before you start your garden—these range from hand tools to oils and soil test kits. The good news is that most of these will only cost you a few dollars each and can be found in almost any garden shop or hardware. But first, we will not be covering the seeds here. If you want to grow a plant, you will have to buy seed or young plant. This should be obvious, and only you know exactly what fruits and vegetables that are interested in growth. If you have not known, we will be covering fruits, vegetables, and herbs in chapters four, five, and six.

As plants grow, it is they need to take care of them, and health maintenance tools mean. But if you want your plants to grow at all, you will have to water them. You have three options for this. The first is to get yourself a shower and use that. While using a watering can, simply makes it easier to pour water, many people enjoy using, as they give the feeling of being a "real" gardener. You can just as easily save your money and use a measuring cup or even a single cup to drink. Just remember to keep the glass garden separated from the babies since there are times when you need to add nutrients to your plant's water would not mind consumed yourself directly! By last,

To adjust and maintain the plants as they grow, they will need to obtain various types of hand tools. First is a set of pruning shears. You will have to cut their plants at specific points to promote healthy growth or delete infected limbs. You can use a scissor assembly, but they can create a rough

Cut, which would harm your plant. Every time the plants are cut, they receive a shock to your system. A good set of scissors will ensure that the cuts that cause the least damage. Also you want to get a small rake to the ground and a palette, although these are not as important as the scissors. What is essential is that a shovel is achieved. You want to be able to dig beneath the roots, especially when they are young, and you have to move your boat from planting to the increasingly large pot.

While you will more than likely you are with scissors to remove unhealthy tips, the best option available to us gardeners is to prevent infection or infestation before it happens. We have already talked about some ways to do this before, but another effective way is to buy a little neem oil. Neem oil is made out of natural chemicals that are vegetable oil pressure fruit and herb neem seeds. These chemicals are used to deter pests like mites and fight infectious diseases and fungi. You can buy at almost any garden center and should be applied to the plants once a week. Since it is more cost-effective than neem oil in buying pour bottles, also you want to get a spray bottle from your local dollar store. This is one of those purchases that many indoor gardeners assume they will not need,

Although you will need to have a thermometer to read the temperature of the growing area, you also want a soil thermometer to have a clear idea of how your plants are doing. You can always get one and use it to test the soil of its various pots occasionally. However, most are cheap enough that it makes more sense only to purchase for each container and leave in place so that you can always check the temperature of the soil at a glance. Speaking of the earth, it is a good idea to get a testing kit so you can check the pH level of the pots. The pH level gives you an understanding of nutrients and the chemical balance of the soil. Most plants want to be between 5.5 and 7.5, right of most middle of that range. Test kits tend to come with various applications, but run out quickly.

Once you have these tools, you will have all the essentials needed to take their first plants from seed to harvest. As you become accustomed to working with its interior garden, it is likely to discover new tools that will make your life easier, but these can be purchased as the need arises.

CHAPTER 3:

The Operation Cycle
Of A Garden Indoor

N ow that you have everything you need for your garden, it's time to put everything together and get your hands dirty! Since the most common way that gardeners start out is by planting seeds, let's start with a look at how to raise our fruits and vegetables from seed to seedling and then transplant them from the container planting containers that have established for a proper garden. From there, we will move on to the rest of the operating cycle, aspects such as irrigation and fertilization of plants.

With the knowledge in this chapter, you will know what happens in raising their plants. Then the next three chapters will be on fruits, vegetables, and herbs, respectively. These chapters each focus on the type of plant in question and go into detail about them there. However, all plants analyzed in the following chapters are raised correctly, the operating cycle established in this chapter.

Dirtying pots to plant your garden

In the last chapter, we saw two ways to make our own potting soil. Of course, you can always go to your garden center and buy pre-made land to the local pots, so the choice of which to use is completely up to you. Whatever you go with, however, you are going to do more or less the same with him. Fill the containers intended to be a part of your garden so that the soil is a quarter inch from the edge of the pot. Since we are starting with seeds, which is fine that the only concern fills the smallest pots to be used for seedlings at this stage. Just remember that your seedlings were transferred to larger pots when they are large enough,

Now that the pots are ground, it's time to turn your attention to the seeds you want to plant. Assuming you have already bought the seeds you want from your local garden center, just could explode in their packages and call it a day. But it's always a better idea to help their seeds through the germination process through a little extra work. This is especially true if you are planting the seeds with a hard shell, like sweet peas or spinach. You can help your plants to germinate by using one of the following three methods.

The first approach is the use of scarification. In order to help the hard shell of the seed decompose properly, take garden scissors bought and scrape the skin with them. You do not want to create any deep scratches to expose the inside of the shell as this can ruin the seed, just want

Slightly damage the exterior to be a little weaker. Another way to do this is to take some sandpaper and gently rub the seed to dilute the shell. If you go with the approach of scarification, then you will need to plant these seeds as soon as you finish.

Stratification offers another approach that can help with hard-shelled seeds, although they are most often used for outside plant varieties of fruits, vegetables, or herbs. However, some plants such as lettuce or peas perennial sweet benefit greatly from stratification. These seeds tend to be chemical substances present, which makes germination difficult or even impossible. In order to get through the hard shell, you need to use a combination of cold and warm temperatures. The best way to accomplish this is to let the first seeds soak for 24 hours in water. The end of the soak period, remove seeds and put them in a resealable plastic bag with a little peat moss or vermiculite and then paste in a refrigerator.

The third method is the easiest, and that is to soak the seeds. The seeds benefit from soaking are those with hard layers such as asparagus, carrots, corn, peas, pumpkins, or squash, to name a few. While these seeds can continue to grow without the soaking process, it could take days or weeks to germinate this way. Soak the seeds, simply place in a little warm water for 12 to 24 hours. When you return to your seeds, you may notice that some of them are now floating. These can be thrown away because it is unlikely to germinate properly. Those who still sit quietly at the bottom of the water will be those plants. Remove the seeds and rinse with clean water. We do this to eliminate chemicals that are released during the soaking process. Plant these seeds as soon as you finish rinsing.

Now that you have or soft shell seeds ready to plant seeds or hard shells that have been prepared correctly, it's time to plant in their containers. Create a small hole for your seeds; it is between a quarter and half of an inch deep. You can have more than one hole in a container, as long as there is enough room to keep about an inch apart. Drop a couple of seeds in

Each of the holes he has done and then covered with soil. You do not want land covering to be too tight, as this will make it more difficult for oxygen to reach the seeds, and this can cause your plants to drown. You may not want to make the holes too deep. Otherwise, seedlings may be unable to leave at the top. When a seed germinates, the shell is broken, and the young plant uses this energy to dig their way out of the earth. If it is too deep, then they do not have enough vitality to exit. You may want to cover the container with some plastic wrap in order to maintain moisture and humidity levels up. Keeping these containers in a hot area,

Although it can be somewhat tedious at this stage, it is in your best interest to keep an eye on your plants every day. Most of the time, there will be nothing to see, just a bowl with a little dirt on it. But before long, it will realize a small stem protruding from the earth. Then they are derived; it will begin to grow branches and leaves. Once you detect these sheets will be time to transfer the plant in a larger container. We do this because the root system of the plant will run out of room to grow in these small containers that will prevent growth and even possibly kill the plant.

Transfer their plants to the new container; the first step is to decide which plants will move. Because you planted several seeds in these first pots, you need to ensure stronger transplanting seedlings. See what plant is growing - this will be to transfer. You will need to transfer to a plant used container. So if you made three holes in their packaging and dropped the seeds in the three, it will move the strongest of the three and leave the other two behind. Put your hand over the cup and extend your fingers to plant seedling stands between two fingers. Slowly turn the pot to the soil begins to fall, but the remains of plants against your hand. You want the plant roots to remain in his hand. Fill half of the new container with the same potting soil (always use the same. Otherwise, the sudden change will shock plant), place the plant on the ground, and add more. You want the rootball to be only one or two inches of the top of the container; This is done so that there is enough space for the roots to continue to grow. If you already have a container filled with earth, then you just have to dig a hole large enough to place the plant. Add This is done so that there is enough space for the roots to continue to grow. If you already have a container filled with earth, then you just have to dig a hole large enough to place the plant. Add This is done so that there is enough space for the roots to continue to grow. If you already have a container filled with earth, then you just have to dig a hole large enough to place the plant. Add

More soil on top of the plant in order to keep at around the same depth as was in the first container.

If all went well, have, then you will not see any problem, and your plants will continue to grow unhindered. Keep checking on them every day and provide seedlings with temperature, pH level, moisture, and water needs of species to grow. In doing this, you will have fully developed plants at any time.

Fertilize your indoor garden

Humans need to drink and eat. Considering the risk, it is clear that plants also need to drink plenty of fluids. But as the circumstance occurs, plants also need to eat. They only need their nutrients to come from the soil or liquid fertilizer. The plant roots extend below the ground, spreading in order to find more food to provide all the nutrients they need to continue to grow nice and healthy. If you are raising your plants outdoors in the ground, then those roots can stretch a good distance and find lots of nutrients. But raising those same houseplants, there is only so much space in each container can be extended, and there are only so many nutrients in the soil.

Regardless of what potting soil you decide to use, dry your plants suck nutrients in less than two months. When this happens, they will begin to starve. You can save time in this process by adding a slow-release fertilizer or manure pellets (like chicken) on the floor. However, these are only going to buy your plants a certain amount of breathing space. They will not be sufficient by themselves to keep their plants starve. To do this, they will need to create a regular schedule to feed your plants a liquid fertilizer. There are many liquid fertilizers available on the market that can be purchased, or you can make your own. We will see how to make our own in a moment, but before doing so,

your plants. An obtaining an understanding of this, you have the best possible understanding of what they need.

Most available fertilizers are mainly focused on providing three plant nutrients nitrogen, phosphorus, and potassium, or NPK. I say that most fertilizers because there is a decent amount on the market these approaches in only one of these three nutrients instead of three. You can also purchase these nutrients on their own in a solid form intended to be dissolved in water. However, if you are buying pre-made fertilizer for your indoor garden, then the best idea is to choose a fertilizer that has an NPK ratio with equal amounts of each nutrient. Of course, it rarely is always a relation one to one, and so is well that the relationship is a bit irregular, provided that the nutrients are present in approximately equal amounts. If you are growing plants fruit or fruit such as strawberries, raspberries, tomatoes, or peppers, then they will want to use a fertilizer with a higher amount of potassium as this helps plants to grow their fruits properly. When a purchased fertilizer used in the store, you should always follow the instructions on the package to avoid overfeeding. When they overfeed, the pH level in the soil is raised too high levels. If you purchased soil test kits or electronic reader pH, then you should keep a close eye on the pH level. Then they will want to use a fertilizer with a higher amount of potassium as this helps plants to grow their fruits properly. When a purchased fertilizer used in the store, you should always follow the instructions on the package to avoid overfeeding. When they overfeed, the pH level in the soil is raised too high levels. If you purchased soil test kits or electronic reader pH, then you should keep a close eye on the pH level. Then they will want to use a fertilizer with a higher amount of potassium as this helps plants to grow their fruits properly. When a purchased fertilizer used in the store, you should always follow the instructions on the package to avoid overfeeding. When they overfeed, the pH level in the soil is raised too high levels. If you purchased soil test kits or electronic reader pH, then you should keep a close eye on the pH level.

Buying fertilizer can quickly become expensive if you have a large garden to maintain. One way to avoid this is the increasing cost of making your own. But keep in mind that it is always a very bad process! One way to quickly get a little fertilizer is to fill a bag with compost and leave it to soak in water for ten days. On the tenth day, water is added to the mixture until the color changes from black to gray slightly as tea, time that is ready to use. Another simple urine fertilizer used as the main ingredient, as it is sterile, has a good amount of potassium, and a lot of nitrogen in it, and is very easy to acquire, since you can use your own! Dilute one part urine forty parts water, and yourself a quick and efficient fertilizer. However, although this method is a bit more difficult, you may be interested in making a comfrey fertilizer because of its high concentration of potassium. The same steps taken to make a comfrey fertilizer can be used to make fertilizer nettle borage or if a count greater nitrogen.

Comfrey is a European grass having high levels of potassium, phosphorus, and nitrogen. That means that this herb can provide all you need from an NPK fertilizer. There are ways to turn this into a fertilizer well, but you need to bear in mind that what is really good comfrey is that you can grow by itself as part of your herb garden so you can always have a lot of material home to become fertilizer. It is more or less one of the best investments you can make when it comes to feeding your plants. When there is too much carbon in a bed plant, this can make it difficult for plants to get the best benefits of nitrogen in the soil.

Comfrey compost, all you need do is stuff a bunch of comfrey leaves in a large bowl. Cutting a small hole in the bottom of the vessel and put under a small bowl to catch the liquid dripping black. A couple of weeks to start producing this liquid black is needed, although it may be accelerated by using a heavy object to press down on the leaves. This liquid is excellent for fertilizer when mixed with water at a ratio of 15: 1. That's all it takes to make fertilizer comfrey, but there is more you can do with comfrey around your garden. Take after pressure leaves and use them to feed their potatoes or tomatoes as nutritious mulch. While letting comfrey leaves wilt during the first day, which can be used in this way, you can also add comfrey leaf to containers that are planning to use than to add more nutrients to the initial ground. Make sure you are using slightly older plants and no young seedlings as they may be too strong for them and lead to burn nutrients. Finally, you can add comfrey leaves to your compost to help make it more nutritious because it can be too strong for them and lead to burn nutrients. Finally, you can add comfrey leaves to your compost to help make it more nutritious because it can be too strong for them and lead to burn nutrients. Finally, you can add comfrey leaves to your compost to help make it more nutritious.

If you purchased your subscription, then you instructions on how often to use it, and you should always listen to these instructions. However, if you created your account, then you will need to educate yourself on the needs of particular plants you are looking for food. Some, like fruiting vegetables like tomatoes or peppers, will benefit from a weekly feeding program. However, there are others, such as lettuce, which do not need regular supply fertilizer. You should always investigate their plants before planting, either by searching for Google information or ask your local garden center employees. Furthermore, it should not try to fertilizer plants that are highly stressed out. While

It may seem a good idea to dispense with fertilizers to help them get better, and it is actually much less stressful for the plant to clean water instead will. Also, you do not need to use liquid fertilizer in your herbs because they generally grow best as the light in nutrients.

Watering your plants

While it is one of the most vital parts of tending to any garden, watering the garden inside, it is a straightforward process. But since they are growing fruits and vegetables, it is worth noting that irrigation is even more critical than if you were growing flowers. This is because when you let go dry, vegetable plants will produce a weak harvest and also can ruin the whole crop. Therefore, if there is a part of the operating cycle that you can not ignore, which is to ensure that your plants are adequately watered. But this is not an excuse to drown your plants by overwatering them either; You need to be aware of when their water.

Your plants will need to be watered often, much more often than the same type of plant would require if grown on land to the outdoors. This is because potting soil tends to dry much faster than the soil in your backyard. You also need to be aware of the temperature; in the days

Which the temperature rises, you need more water (sometimes even several times in one day). If you are not sure whether or not it is time to water the plants, there are two ways you can see if they are ready. The first is to put your finger on the ground. Should fit your finger deep enough that the joint of the middle phalanx plunges into the earth, this is the main joint in the digit after the knuckle. If the soil is dry, then you want to water. The other way to check is to lift the container or slightly tilted to the side. Try to do this the first time you water the plants and later for follow up. You will notice that the container is much lighter when dry,

You need to make sure that you water your plants thoroughly. When potting soil is dry, it can be a bit of a pain so effectively water itself. Sometimes the root ball away from the sides of the container when dry, and this creates a situation that watering the plant, all the water goes down the hands of the container chops roots left behind. You can get around this problem, always watering your plants so that the level of the water rises to the top of the container. Doing this ensures the roots of your plant to get plenty of water. However, this can easily lead to choking the plant, so it is worth seeing the ground first to make sure it is the right time for water.

Note that there is a difference between dry soil and wet soil. A finger is removing the potting mix, moist soil sticking to it. If this happens, then there is no time to water. While vegetable plants should never be left to dry, it's an excellent idea always to read the instructions that come with the seeds and ask an employee at your local garden center. Browse reliable internet sites for best practice care for that species. Different plants have different water needs, so always inquire about the needs of your plant rather than take what is best for them.

Pruning your plant

An important, but often overlooked gardening is pruning.

Many people are afraid to cut your plant, but it is quite easy and is not harmful to the plant. This section will be brief, but cover the important aspect of pruning and how it is suitable for your plant.

Most plants benefit in some way, shape, or form of regular pruning. In many plants, cutting back really help grow the plant. It's a bit ironic that push back the plant can make it grow bigger!

It is also essential for growing healthy, pest-free plants. Dead or dying parts of plants are more susceptible to pest infestation unwanted then spread to the healthy parts of the plant. By eliminating problem areas that can help prevent errors is rooted in the first place. While growing indoors, pests are much less likely, but do not underestimate their determination to destroy your plants!

Pruning is also a way to maintain the size of the plant under control. If a plant is growing too big for your taste and then merely cutting back will not damage the plant and help keep him in line with his vision. Bonsai trees are a great example of this; there is an art all pruning and maintenance of the plant.

 Knowing when to prune or harvest a plant is sometimes tricky. Note that, even when done incorrectly, it is rarely fatal to plants. It can cause small sizes of flower crops or for a while, but the plant is likely to survive. This is even more true in the interior, where a sudden cold snap is not expected to happen, so do not be afraid to mess up.

A pruning always use tools sharp and clean. It is cutting into the skin of the plant and plant exposure to potential infections from the outside world. To maintain it's clean the tools that help keep your plants healthy.

For general purposes, generally, you want to do pruning in the late winter before the growing season of plants. Doing so during the growing season could potentially eliminate or prevent unopened buds growth if too long ago.

That said, do not be afraid to make some general maintenance for classification or aesthetic reasons. This should also include the systematic removal of dead or dying parts of plants. Since there is no risk of a fallen leaf budding, eliminating these must be the year to do. Just be careful not to remove growing or budding follows that if you're looking to harvest later.

If you notice pests, then it is also smart to prune the infected parts of the plant. This help can prevent pests from spreading and keep the rest of your healthy plant. You are going to sacrifice some but keeps the package.

However, this only works if you notice pests before they spread too. Later, we will see how to deal with pests.

Harvesting fruits, vegetables, and herbs are a bit easier.

You can still make the same type of pruning process to keep under control, but

The actual edible parts of the plant should be harvested when ripe. This depends on the type of plant and your taste at various maturity levels, sometimes slightly different flavors.

Now for some things to avoid. When harvesting or pruning, always careful not to cut too deep root or the stem. The goal of pruning is to reduce the plant but not kill him. A leaving intact, the sources can be sure that the plant will grow healthy and happy.

You're. Also, they do not want to be too enthusiastic about pruning. A little here and there is fine, but remember that you are removing parts of the plant growth and should do so in moderation.

Pruning is generally not severe and is essential for plant growth. Most gardeners are so afraid to prune your plants back a little, but in most cases, there is little chance that you're going to hurt the plant. Since indoor plants are protected from the elements, including some over-pruning is not likely to cause permanent damage. Remember, some pruning goes a long way to help your plant stay healthy and look beautiful.

Pest Control

Like it or not, part of gardening is dealing with the possibility of unwanted pests. These usually come in the form of insects that can damage or kill your plants, not to mention being unsightly at home. In this section, we will look at how to prevent pests, common indoor pests that can be seen, and how to remove them if you do them.

Fortunately, with a few simple steps that can significantly reduce the risk of infestation. As the saying goes, "A good defense is a great offense," which is correct for pest control. A preventive taking measures before they appear insects can potentially prevent the problem completely.

While in the growing interior makes alleviate much of the risk, plants are no completely safe way infestation. There are still plenty of opportunities for annoying insects to attack your plants.

You are at higher risk if you let them out of their encampment at all or grow out in the summer but winter in the garden. In these situations, you'll want to pay extra close attention to your plants for signs of pests.

With that out of the way, let's take a look at some of the ways you can help keep your plants will become a home for pests in the first place.

Daily monitor

The biggest thing you can do to prevent an infestation is to monitor your plants as often as possible. Make a quick control over land and look for visible signs of errors every day or two is the first line of defense against these pesky bugs. This should be fairly simple if you are already checking to see if the plants need to be watered.

Giving greater distance are the insects themselves, but other signs may include discoloration, holes in the leaves, or other damage to the plant. Always give the underside of the leaves again too. There are many types of common insects like to cluster at the bottom of the leaves. As before catching insects, the easier it is to get rid of them.

Good supervision is the easiest way to keep your plants free of pests. It is not uncommon for large infestations pop-up overnight, so we will probably be able to catch them before they grow too large. As you might be able to guess, it's much easier to deal with a small number of errors when their numbers grow too large.

Use clean containers

Always take a while for new clean containers with soap and warm water your plants before moving them. This is especially true if purchased in a place with a lot of different plants; this is a culture broth potential for insects. This includes many big box hardware stores, especially if the containers are stored outside in a garden section. A quick wash with warm water and soap will be sufficient to remove unwanted visitors.

This is also important if you move your plants outdoors during the summer months. Give wash containers quickly before bringing back at home. This helps stop any bugs or their eggs stuck to the plant during the summer to keep indoors during the winter.

Promptly remove dead leaves or branches

To monitor the health of your plant also helps keep the bugs away. If any dead or dying parts trim them back is observed. This also includes dead leaves or stems that can be present in the soil. Many types of insects thrive on the weakened plant. Take a look at the above types of pruning for information on how to reduce your plant back safely.

Common pests
Here is a common indoor couple of mistakes to consider.

Whiteflies

Look for the black, sticky film that looks almost like mold. As they mature, resemble small white flies, hence its name. When disturbed,
 They fly through the air. Feed by sucking plant nutrients that cause growth retardation and weak plants.

Aphids

Often green, but they come in other colors too. They are grouped at the bottom of the sheets, so be sure to check here. Secrete a sticky substance that is sweet and can attract more insects like ants. They also feed on the plant, causing the leaves to wilt and a general lack of health of the plant as a whole.

Scale

Small and brown, cluster on the undersides of the leaves or the stem.
It looks almost more like small shells that insects sometimes. Take care of them in the branches, and that can be difficult to

detect before they become a big problem. His brown mix allows quite easily to be sure to give your plant stems a critical eye to prevent this plague go unnoticed.

Mealybugs

Fluffy and white, they look almost like cotton or the remains of a great lion. They can be found in all parts of plants, but generally.

They are under the leaves to the beginning. Having them appear in other places often be signs of a larger infestation.

Spider mites

These pests are usually too small to be seen without some sort of magnifying glass. Look for discoloration of the leaves, which is a telltale sign of their precedence. A growing number also can be noticed, a very thin film between the leaves and branches of the plants that looks almost like a spider web. These are not really a bug, but a type of arachnid.

I have an infestation, and now what?

So you have been determined to have some pests, and now it's time to get rid of them. As with anything, the method will depend on the problem. Let's take a look at some solutions to common errors.

Eliminate the problem

If you are lucky enough to catch an early infestation, it may be possible to simply remove the affected area. If errors are located in one area of the disposal plant, an area that can stop the infestation. Your

They catch it early, however, and unfortunately, many mistakes can spread very quickly throughout the plant.

beneficial insects

Some errors are actually good for your garden and eat that causing damage. One very popular "beneficial insects" is the common ladybug. Ladybugs protect your garden and keep away from eating different varieties of pests. They themselves do not cause damage to plants, so it is perfectly fine to bring them into your garden as a natural insect repellent. If you find them, of course, it is best to leave them alone, because it is likely keeping the most dangerous pests away.

Soapy water

A very easy and natural repellant to do is just mix some dishwashing soap with water in a small spray bottle. This mixture was shown to repel insects certain types while being safe to plants. Also, it does not use harmful chemicals and is very quick to do. If you find errors in your plants, this is a good first step to try.

Natural pesticides

If the soapy water does not work, then there are a variety of natural pesticides that have been proven to keep the bugs away. These are products such as neem oil derived from natural plants having pesticidal properties. Which of these you get depends on the type of error? For example, the above neem oil is great for getting rid of cochineal. There are other repellents available for different types of pests.

Overall, it is important not to panic. Do a little research for the pest, and figure out the best way to remove it. Most insects are not too difficult to remove, so with a little effort of your plants will return to their animated Self.

CHAPTER 4:

Beautiful Fruit Growing

Everything you need to know about maintaining your garden has already been covered, so now is the time to get in the plants themselves finally. They are the first fruits, plants tastiest of all. You will learn what it takes to grow plants healthy fruits with high yields. There is not enough space in this book to cover every type of fruit, so I stay at some of the most popular ways to see exactly what is going to raise strawberries, peaches, and delicious.

Just a note: While tomatoes are technically a fruit, we will be looking at them in the next chapter. Add vegetables for a salad, not a fruit punch, after all!

Why Organic foods are better

Organic farming has become a hot trend these days, more and more people are jumping on board the ecological train. But natural is more than a fad that will eventually pass. There are numerous benefits to grow and eat these foods rather than pumping your garden (and your dinner table), full of every kind of believable chemistry. The benefits of organic fruit and products are more recognizable in the broader field of agriculture and industry movements. However, there are many benefits further down the chain that beneficially affects people who eat these foods. Let's take a look at these pictures.

The main thing that separates organic food from the rest is the lack of chemicals. No harmful transgenic used for organic growth. This is great because many genetically modified organisms are used along with other toxic chemicals in modern agricultural practices these days. Buying organic food supports farmers who care about the long-term consequences of the food they produce and withdraw money from the hands of organizations willing to jeopardize their health for profit. It also reinforces the healthiest soil, reduces the growth of super strains, saves taxpayer money (in the form of subsidies for non-organic farmers), and keeps harmful chemicals to seep into the oceans. But, what are the benefits of organic farming that provides as an indoor gardener? Strictly speaking, there are four answers to this question.

The first benefit is the taste. A plant underlined tastes terrible - it's just a fact. A lot of GMOs produce crops that are under stress, and you can tell the difference when a ripe fruit OGM one who has been compared.

Organically grown. Stressed plants need to spend energy to repair themselves and finding more nutrients. Meanwhile, a healthy plant organic farming can concentrate its strength in producing the best fruit possible. That, in turn, means juicier, more abundant fruits, vegetables tastier, and (!), And this is terrific news for your taste buds.

Organic foods also have more nutrients and antioxidants than those grown by chemical processes. Therefore, the fruits are grown organically in your apartment will be super high for you and your health. Additional nutrients come from the land that is used in organic farming. We aim to use natural compost and fertilizer to keep our rich potting soil nutrients for our fruits and vegetables, and this shows its benefits in the nutrient content of the fruit we produce. Fruit developed organically typically has 30% more antioxidants compared to products grown GMO. That is a considerable increase when it is remembered that organic fruit also tastes better. Not only feel better, but it is better for you,

Growing organic food promotes a healthier lifestyle in general. I believe that, when you see how the food is of your taste indoor garden, you will agree. Many gardeners like to share their harvest with family and friends, and this, in turn, spreads joys of organic farming to more people. Once people have experienced much more delicious are its fruits, which are much more likely to reach for next time they have organically grown produce shopping. That means more money flowing into healthy agricultural practices that promote wellness.

Also, when you are building your fruit, which can not help but become much more involved in what you put in your body,

Finally, organic fruits and vegetable growing will teach you about the number of other products that may go. Most people toss out your compost and do not spend a second thinking about how they could use it.

Once you start saving your fertilizer for their crops and studying how you can make use of their plants (such as the many advantages of comfrey), you will realize that there are many more uses for the products around you than imagined previously. These factors promote a more sustainable way of life and get both use things around them as possible. While this may seem a strange reason

Promote organic fruit; this subtle shift in perspective is bound to have a significant impact on the carbon footprint and how you consider waste.

Strawberries

Strawberries could not be one of the first things that come to mind as easy to grow indoors, but it is much easier than most people think. The increasing interior has the benefits of fewer pests, which has always been the ruin of strawberry growers. One of the main concerns of the strawberry is space. Strawberries need plenty of room to grow, so they can not begin to mold. The use of hanging baskets or

The vertical shelf is a great way to pack a lot of plants in a smaller area. Unfortunately, if you do not have a lot of space, strawberries' growth might not be a perfect option for you.

Strawberries need the least 6 hours of direct sunlight a day. Less and the plant does not work as well, and the fruit will not be as delicious. It also runs the risk of them no fruit at all.

Check the strawberries for daily water needs. If the soil is dry, give them some water. Fruits have a shallow root system, so it is essential to be on both irrigated, and its roots will not be able to absorb water as it flows more rooted into the ground.

Strawberries can be a little tricky to get the hang of, but once you get into the groove are not so challenging to grow. The main concern is to have ample space for the roots to spread. If you can set below are an excellent choice to grow!

Tomatoes

Tomatoes are generally a plant to the outside but can be grown indoors as well. It is no longer produced in the winter months; the cold environments need to grow indoors to produce this fruit throughout the year. Note that while healthy, tomatoes grown indoors are smaller than their cousins to the outdoors.

Tomatoes need full sun or light for at least 8 hours a day. This is something you should not skimp on what is the key to growing vegetables.

Many people have difficulty even outdoors with tomato lighting, which may be wise to invest in some grow lights if you plan on building this plant inside.

Another critical factor for the growth of tomato is temperature. Keep the area around tomatoes at the least 65 degrees Fahrenheit. Also, be very careful not to expose them to cold drafts or blasts, especially in the winter months, as this can quickly kill the plant or prevent flowering.

Keep the soil moist for optimal growth. If the ground begins to dry, give your plants a little water. Tomatoes are a bit shaky in their growth, and leaving the field too dry for too long can spell disaster.

Tomatoes It can be tricky to grow at. First, the most important thing to consider is lighting needs. Those who do not receive enough light will not produce edible fruit. If you can get that down, then the rest is pretty straightforward.

CHAPTER 5:

Delicious Vegetable Crops

A lthough fruits, thanks to its natural sugars, are the sweetest plants can grow indoors, most gardeners in our position, is primarily interested in growing vegetables, Why? Well, they are versatile and provide tons of nutritional value. We have seen that fruits organically grown produce more nutritious crops; when this increase in performance combined with health benefits that come from eating a lot of vegetables, it is easy to see why growing your plants is a great option. But it is not only healthy but also super fun!

The best part of growing vegetables indoors is no low season. You can have delicious tomatoes and cucumbers even during the harshest winters. Plants will not grow on the ground when there are ten centimeters of snow covering it but certainly grow in home settings. Many of the vegetables you buy at the supermarket during the winter are expensive, although they may be inferior products. With its interior garden, it never has to be overcharged for less than perfect vegetables again. So let's turn our attention to what is needed to raise tomatoes inside (the fruit honestly should have been born a plant!).

Chives

Chives or green onions are a great first plant for indoor growing. In the like scallions, his hard smell can add some natural pest control for your garden. Also, like scallions, chives are quite resilient, making them easy to grow even for beginners.

Chives require about 6 hours of sunshine a day. A council serves to rotate the container every few days to ensure that all plant receives the same light.

Chives, once again, as the soil moist, but not soggy. If you grow from seeds, you can provide some water before and just after germination but cut a little as they age, and the rate of growth decreases.

Overall, scallions are quite easy to grow. In the like Chives are very strong and difficult to kill. They are also fairly standard for the van plants according to their needs, so many pieces of gardening wisdom generic apply to them.

Eggplants

Although a little smaller in size, when grown indoors, doing so is an excellent choice for those, who love eggplant. Inside, you have complete control.

Environmental and temperature-sensitive plants such as eggplant This makes it easier for their growth. Said this is probably the most difficult element in this list to grow.

One important thing to consider is your space needs. Eggplants are quite large, as is its root systems. Be sure to choose a suitable container and a large space in which to grow them. Like strawberries, this is not a plant for the space-conscious gardener.

It is also important that eggplants are slow-growing. Do not be discouraged if it takes months to grow an adequate sample. There is nothing wrong with what you're doing; just aubergines take a while to mature.

For light, make sure you get 12-14 hours of sunlight a day. Most people need some type of supplemental light in order to meet these needs, so keep this mind before growing.

Water is also a major concern. A problem with eggplants is often the roots to dry and not enough to get water. Do not be afraid to add a little extra water before the soil is dry.

Eggplants are not for the faint of heart! Their needs are at the top in all categories and can be quite difficult to cultivate. For beginners, it is probably a bad first choice, but for those looking to challenge worth the effort.

CHAPTER 6:

Healthy Planting Herbs

While fruits and vegetables can quickly come to mind when considering an interior garden, one should not overlook the value of cultivating your own herbs. Many gardeners get into first indoor gardening starting a small herb garden. They are easy to care for and do not take up much space. Of course, you can always expand the size of an herb garden so much space, but if compared to peach trees or eggplant, these small plants are downright tiny.

But they provide more than its fair share of flavor and aroma. While a herb garden will not put a meal on your dinner table, which will make the food taste fantastic on that plate. In this chapter, we will see the growth of a couple of the most common and versatile herbs. But before I do, let's first turn our attention to what these herbs to make such a compelling addition to any interior garden.

Scallion

Chives are an increasingly popular choice, as they are used in a large number of recipes and taste delicious. T
here are actually two types of chives, garlic chives, and scallion's common onion. Care is the same, but the taste is a

little different if you look at the names that you can easily find the difference.

For lighting, chive needs 6-8 hours of full sun. If lack sufficient light from natural sources, fluorescent light placed 6-12 inches help supplement the plant. A quick, chive note will continue to grow with less light, but not so quickly.

Chives are higher indoors should be watered once the top of the soil is dry to the touch. They also enjoy humid environments. Misting with water can help keep humidity down too much and keep them hydrated and without risk of overwatering.

Chive flavor has also been shown to keep pests under control. Their garlic or onion smell is sharp enough to provide some natural protection from pests. It's pretty rare to see pests chive goal. In fact, scallion placement near other plants shown to slightly reduce your chances of being targeted pest.

One thing to note is that onions are very fast growers and will take care of the container-grown. Therefore, they should not be grown.

 In a common pot, and must give their own space that does not care to be exclusively chive.

Overall, scallions are fairly easy to grow since they are extremely difficult to kill. Even the most careless gardener will have a hard time with chive die in them. They make an excellent first floor to begin to grow.

Coriander

Coriander is another common herb, although it may be a little harder to grow than other herbs. Cilantro is also seen as being much tastier when fresh, so it's really great to add a little flavor to a dish. One thing to keep in mind is that the cilantro not transplant well when a plant is likely where it will remain.

Cilantro needs about four hours of sunshine a solid day with periods of light and shadow degraded later. This makes it a little easier than other plants as a window that only gets sun for a while on a perfect day for it. Too much sun sill actually frying the plant and leave with a wilted appearance and brown.

Cilantro requires good attention to the water in order for proper growth. Like many other plants, soil and check if dry provide water. This should be done frequently as coriander is very nutritious hunger, and leaving it without water can cause growth problems. To the sure to do thorough watering, water should start to leak out the drainage holes.

Overall, cilantro is a bit of a difficult plant to do well because of their aggressive needs nutrients. It is well worth it, though, as fresh cilantro is delicious.

Basil

Basil is grown outdoors, but indoors can be grown equally easily. Basil is a very aromatic herb and can provide useful both in the kitchen and the smell in the home.

Basil needs about six hours of sun a day. If getting from artificial, fluorescent lights, then it takes more or less ten different levels of each they can be used without causing growth problems.

One key thing to consider with basil is that it has a very high tolerance to water stress. The soil should be moist but never soggy. Prolonged exposure to soggy soil rots the roots and kill the plant. Unlike previous chives, basil will die much more quickly if it is not watered properly.

Basil is also known that a producer is very fast and aggressive. It is generally a good idea to keep it in your own pot to prevent them from carrying nutrients from its neighbor. The plan transplant to facilitate continued growth unless start in a container large enough. Basil does such a transplant, so this is not too big of a concern.

In general, basil is the middle of the road in terms of difficulty. It can be a bit difficult to get the right irrigation, but because of its rapid growth it can get

For being a little lax sometimes.

CHAPTER 7:

Common Mistakes And How To Avoid

When it comes to gardening, there are a large number of errors that producers are prone to do when they start out. In fact, truth be told, there are many gardeners who follow commit mistakes despite having years of experience acquired. The most common reason is ignorance makes mistakes. Some people simply think that if they can increase carrots, lettuce then can increase, or if they can grow an orange tree, then they understand how to take care of mint. This attitude ignores the subtle (and not so subtle) differences between plants, and simply reduces a broad topic in the formula too rigid. When this happens, dead plants and crop failures are likely to follow.

While most likely mistakes of their own during the early stages of creating your fruit, vegetable, or indoor herb garden in this chapter is to put both errors more common than new producers are likely to do. Being aware of these errors, reduce your level of ignorance and increases your chances of avoiding their own. Now, this means not tell you, by default, to avoid these mistakes simply because you read this chapter. But it does mean that you have the knowledge to avoid them, as long as you act on it. In the world increasingly, much like life in general, we are obliged to act in our knowledge if we want to see the best results.

Do your research

we have looked at a handful of plants throughout the book, and although some of them share similarities (such as thyme and rosemary), they all have notable differences in the amount of light, water, fertilizer, space, and moisture they want, and the nutrients they like best, and what level of pH they need to stay healthy. If this can be a big difference between the small handful that we were able to see, then you can only imagine how much variety there is in the entire plant kingdom. Not only that, but keep in mind that different subspecies of plants often have their own preferences, although similar, can show a lot of variation. All this adds up to the fact that you should never make an assumption about the needs of a plant.

Instead, do your research on your plants. If you have Internet access, then a quick search on Google will reveal one link after another on how to raise any kind of fruit, vegetable, or herb you are considering. If you are not very tech-savvy, then you should consider stopping at its center and ask local gardening advice. Chances are they will get their seeds from them anyway, why not pick their brains first to find out everything you need to know. Questions to consider they ask are: How often should I water this plant? What type of fertilizer is what they need and how often you need? Does it take long to germinate? How long does it take to grow? When can I expect to start fruiting? The amount of light is what you want? Do you prefer direct light from the sun or partial shade? Than

Should the temperature be maintained? The amount of moisture required? What will pH level need? Is there anything I should know about pollination by hand? Are there health risks you should consider?

Ask questions, and do your research should be the first step you take when considering increasingly something that is new to you. Even before looking at the price of seeds or seedlings, ask all the questions that need answering if you are or are not able to provide an ideal environment for these plants. Be prepared with the information that will save you money as you can avoid those that are not a good choice, and can also save yourself the disappointment of seeing new plant wilt and die.

Growing too much at once

When you are starting out, many people have big, big plans for its interior gardens. They will have the lettuce and tomatoes, carrots and eggplant, a peach, a little rosemary, and a bunch of mints. In theory, this sounds amazing. Who would not want to have much delicious food at your fingertips? But in practice, this is often a recipe for disaster.

The first question that many people are going to run into expanding too fast is the fact that things are not growing as they thought. The fact that you plant a seed does not mean it will grow. It can be particularly daunting for new gardeners when it happens once, but be aware when it happens to several plants, all at the same time. Moreover, even if they do germinate, each plant will grow at different rates, and this means you will have to balance the needs of a number of different plants that are all at different stages of development. Pay special attention to the use of the word "balance." Gardening occupies your time and attention; you need to check your plants to get an idea of how they are doing, then adjust care accordingly.

When you start, start small and then expand as you become more comfortable with the care of a garden. While suggesting from one level, many will find that this is too small to make it worth your time. Yes

Need more, two or three plants are allowed, but limited to this. Collect plants with similar care routines and environmental requirements for you to worry about building an environment, rather than making several points. Take these plants to harvest before adding more. In this way, you know what is required for each step in the process of care. Start slowly and add more as your skill and increases understanding. Approach it with a sensible attitude. Seen in this way, become a gardening expert, it is not so different from any other skill.

Sowing seeds too close together

When you are first putting the seeds or seedlings (even) in a container, it will seem like there is a lot of space. After all, the seeds are super small, and so you can put a whole beat them in a container without you feeling like they are moving together. While this is true in these early stages of growth, quickly it comes to regret this decision when plants begin to grow, and you realize you have no space at all. But why is this a bad thing, necessarily?

First, while you will notice the lack of space at the top of the floor, which is really what is happening on the ground that is damaging your plants a maximum, their roots will begin to snarl and fight to find their own space as they grow, and this will cause a number of problems that negatively affect their overall health. Those same roots will have to compete with each other for nutrients, and this means that all plants will be much less healthy compared to those who get all the nutrients they need without a fight. The struggle to fight for nutrients energy waste, an energy that would be better used in promoting growth. Plants with delayed growth are planted as a result of being too close together.

Another factor to consider is that pests and diseases can spread more easily from one plant to another when they are too close together. On the other hand, they have more places to hide; it is much more difficult to see all the nooks and crannies of their plants when they are hidden from each other. Therefore it is evident that planting too close together creates more problems with pests and diseases and smaller harvests less tasty food.

No Checking pests or cleaning Disease

Speaking of pests - has been checking them? If not, how do you know that your plants are still healthy? The fact that pests do not see when you look at their plants does not mean it can not be that already feed on plants. There are many signs of infection, such as discoloration of leaves, bumps or holes in the leaves, or leaves that have begun to wilt no discernible reason. The longer an infestation takes hold, the more damage your plants will hold, and can only take so much before they give up and die.

You want to ensure that your plants are free from infestation or infection; the simplest precaution is to check every day. This takes time, this resource that many new producers off when they decide to grow plants too. While many pests can be detected with the naked eye, there are more than a few examples that are hidden or invisible naked eye. If you see pests, you need to start treating your plants immediately. But also specific tests should be done on a daily basis to see if any of these parasites are hidden. Use the rake to check the soil on the roots, as many pests lay their eggs on the ground; the offspring of these eggs are given the opportunity, chewing away at the stem. Then, take a piece of paper towel or toilet paper, and clean the underside of the leaves. If the paper comes out with traces of blood, then there are pests that are going to have to deal with it. There are many methods to deal with pests, but you should do your research before embarking on any of them. Since fruits, vegetables and herbs are all.

Plants that grow with the intention of eating, which is crucial to ensure that any pesticide or solution used to treat your plants the food you eat is not going to hurt.

While you are making a habit of checking for pests, you should also keep your eyes open for signs of disease. White powdery mildew, mold, discoloration, wilting branches, rotten fruit - all these are signs that your plants have caught a disease. The first step in the fight against most diseases is to cut the infected parts and immediately dispose of them to the outdoors. They apply treatments to ensure their plants after these treatments are not harmful to humans.

There are several key steps you should take to prevent disease in the first place. Apply neem oil on a weekly basis, even if there are no signs of infestation or infection. This is a preventive measure that will not have to cope with these annoyances. Also, keep close surveillance on the amount of water and light that plants are increasing to make sure they are not getting too little or too much. Then check the pH level of the soil to make sure they have enough nutrients, as very few can leave them sick, and too many nutrients can cause burns. Last but not least, make sure the dead plant material is removed from the area. The compost used on the floor is fine, but the leaves or branches that have fallen from the plants and rot in the general area are very harmful. This decomposing plant matter, when it is not being used as part of a power system properly planned, can introduce bacteria harmful to their cultivation area. Always be sure to remove any dead plant material or fallen from the growing area and wash your hands before handling your plants.

Conclusion

I n order to properly grow houseplants, you'll have to invest more money in ensuring you have a suitable environment for them. However, much of this money is used in the early parts of the installation, such as purchase grow lights, fans, and humidifiers. Once you have made the investment in this gear, you will be able to reuse again and again for harvest after harvest. Seen this way, the investment becomes easier to justify. Not only that but if you decide to indoor gardening is not for you, then you can resell this equipment to recover some of their money. Just remember to start small when you start; otherwise, the cost of investment and the time you need to make will be much higher.

Creating an indoor garden is no more difficult than growing one to the outdoors. In fact, the level of control we have over an indoor environment makes it easier in many ways. Rain, drought, cold, or snow and half death for your plants, and by using electric lights, which are capable of providing enough "sunlight" to ensure that your plants stay healthy and happy.

As we deal with issues such as global warming and changes in the environment, indoor gardening will continue to grow in popularity. In the future, it seems likely that a substantial proportion of our food will be developed and raised inside, rather than outside. What this means is that the skills and knowledge that have benefited from this book will be more relevant to daily life and more in demand in the coming years. From your indoor garden, today will give you the practical experience you need to teach others how to start yours. Not only is indoor gardening a great choice to enjoy fruits and vegetables grown organically from the comfort of your home, but it is also an investment in you and your family's future.

We have only been able to cover a small selection of plants that can be grown indoors. You should not feel limited to stick to those we have discussed throughout the book. Instead, you should take the lessons we've been here, and apply to fruits, vegetables, herbs and most.

Interest you. Just remember to do your research to make sure you can provide the right environment for your plants, whether blueberries, basil, squash, or anything else. Each plant is unique and should be respected as such. With this attitude and a little care, you will be able to grow anything your heart desires.

So, what are you waiting for? Put this book down and go get your hands dirty tending to her own deck of fruits, vegetables, and herbs Garde

CPSIA information can be obtained
at www.ICGtesting.com
Printed in the USA
BVHW041024071220
595087BV00007B/345